Glass

Sally Morgan and Pauline Lalor

WHY WASTE IT?

SIMON & SCHUSTER
YOUNG BOOKS

△ Remember to warn children that glass is fragile,
△ and is dangerous when it is broken.

WHY WASTE IT? has been researched and compiled by
Simon & Schuster Young Books.   We are very
grateful for the support and guidance provided
by our advisory panel of professional
educationalists in the course of the production.

Advisory panel:
Colin Pidgeon, Headteacher
Wheatfields Junior School, St Albans
Deirdre Walker, Deputy headteacher
Wheatfields Junior School, St Albans
Judith Clarke, Headteacher
Grove Infants School, Harpenden

Commissioning editor: Daphne Butler
Book editor: Claire Llewellyn
Design: M&M Design Partnership
Photographs: Ecoscene except for pages
10, 11, 14 (top and bottom left) Schott
Glass Ltd; page 13 Zefa;
page 14 (bottom right) United Glass;
page 25 (top) Maggie Murray/Format.

First published in Great Britain in 1992
by Simon & Schuster Young Books

Simon & Schuster Young Books
Campus 400, Maylands Avenue
Hemel Hempstead, Herts HP2 7EZ

A catalogue record for this book
is available from the British Library
ISBN 0 7500 1093 2

Printed and bound in Great Britain
by BPCC Hazell Books, Paulton and
Aylesbury

Contents

Most glass is transparent

You can see through most glass.   It is used for windows because it lets in light, but keeps out the weather.

Look round your home for all the things which are made from glass.   Why do you think glass was chosen in each case?

7

Glass is made from sand

Glass has been made for thousands of years.

It is mostly made from sand and two other materials called limestone and soda.   All of these are dug out of the ground from quarries.

Where else might the sand come from?

Sand is heated until it melts

At a glassworks the limestone is crushed to a powder and mixed with the sand and soda.   They are then heated in an oven until they melt into a thick liquid.

The soda helps the sand melt more easily. The limestone makes the glass stronger.

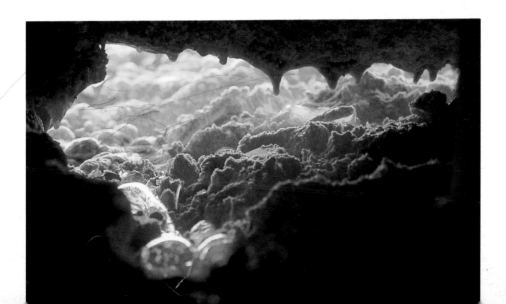

11

You can blow liquid glass

While glass is still liquid, it can be
blown into a bubble, like soapy water,
but it can be made into different shapes.

Glassworkers blow through a long pipe
into a lump of hot glass.   When
they have made the right shape,
they leave the glass to cool.
As it cools, the glass hardens and stays
in that shape for ever – or at least
until it's broken!

What could the man in the picture
be making?

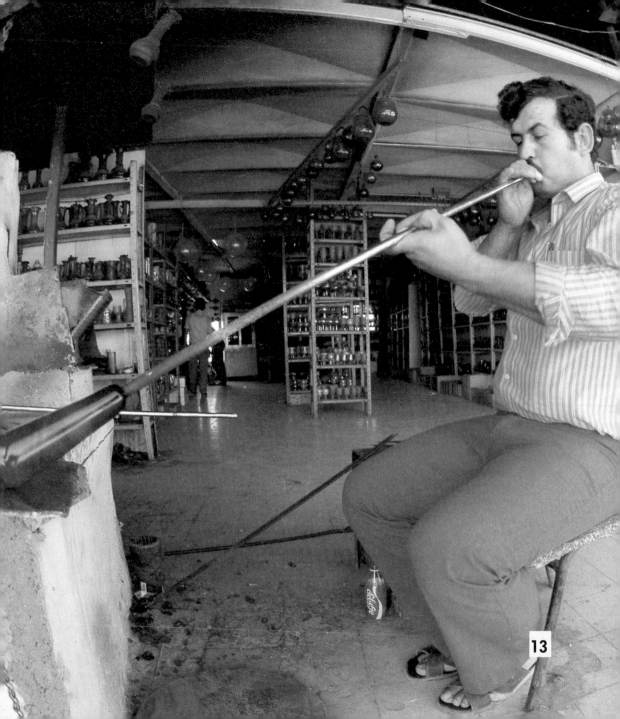

13

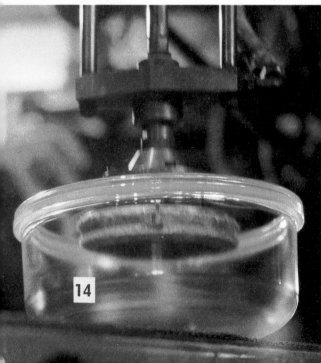

14

Glass is poured into moulds

Have you ever made ice cubes? You pour
water into an ice tray and put it in a
freezer. When the water has frozen hard,
you can turn out the little cubes of ice.
The ice tray was your mould.

It's just the same with glass. Liquid
glass is poured into a mould and left to
cool. As the glass cools, it becomes hard
and keeps the shape of the mould.

What is being made in the pictures?
What else could you use a mould for?

15

Glass makes good containers

Glass containers are made in all shapes and sizes. They are very useful for storing food and drink.

Food in sealed glass jars will stay fresh for a long time. Also, it's easy to see what's inside, and how much you have left.

What do you keep in glass bottles and jars in your home?

17

18

Glass can be reused

Many glass containers are washed clean and used over and over again.   Beer, wine, fizzy drink and milk bottles are all reused in some countries.

You may even get a little money back if you return your old bottles to the shop where you bought them.

Which glass containers do you reuse at home?

Glass can be recycled

Too many people throw away glass bottles
and jars with the rest of their rubbish.
Do you?   This glass could be used again
to make new glass.

Collecting waste glass

In most towns, there are bottle banks where people can take their old glass for recycling.   There are usually separate bins for brown, green and clear glass.

Where are the bottle banks in your town?

23

New glass from old

Lorries take the old glass to a glassworks where it is cleaned and crushed into tiny pieces. The crushed glass is added to the sand when new glass is made.

Old glass melts much more easily than sand. This means that less electricity is needed to heat the ovens.

Do you know why saving electricity is important?

NO HOUSEHOLD GLASS
NO GREENHOUSE GLASS
NO MIRRORS
NO COFFEE TABLE TOP
NO CROCKERY
NO METAL

BOTTLES ONLY

25

Be careful with glass

Glass can break, and when it does, it has very sharp edges.   These can cut people and animals very badly.

Glass never rots away – it is non-biodegradable.   If it is carelessly thrown away, it will lie on the ground until someone moves it.

What would you do if you found some broken glass?

Why recycle glass?

Making new glass means digging more sand, soda and limestone from more quarries.

Quarries are ugly places. If we reuse or recycle old glass, we won't need so many of them.

29

Index